CHANGE YOUR
THINKING,
CHANGE YOUR
LIFE

VANESSA CLARK

CHANGE YOUR
THINKING,
CHANGE YOUR
LIFE

A TIME FOR A CHANGE

ARCHWAY
PUBLISHING

Archway Publishing books may be ordered
through booksellers or by contacting:

Archway Publishing
1663 Liberty Drive
Bloomington, IN 47403
www.archwaypublishing.com
1-(888)-242-5904

Because of the dynamic nature of the Internet, any web addresses or
links contained in this book may have changed since publication and
may no longer be valid. The views expressed in this work are solely those
of the author and do not necessarily reflect the views of the publisher,
and the publisher hereby disclaims any responsibility for them.

Certain stock imagery © Thinkstock.
Any people depicted in stock imagery provided by Thinkstock are
models, and such images are being used for illustrative purposes only.

ISBN: 978-1-4808-0949-9 (e)
ISBN: 978-1-4808-0948-2 (sc)

Library of Congress Control Number: 2014912253

Printed in the United States of America

Archway Publishing rev. date: 8/12/2014

DEDICATION

To my parents, the late Reverend Clyde Hudson and Gessana Hudson, who gave me my foundation in the word of God. They always gave me encouragement, letting me know that I could do whatever I put my mind to do; and constantly told me that what I would do for Christ would last, to have no fear, and to always trust God.

ACKNOWLEDGMENTS

To my sister Sandy Hudson, my best friend, whom I love with all my heart. She has always encouraged me whether I was right or wrong, and has always been there for me. We have laughed together, cried together, and shopped together. At one time, my brother asked us when we were going to get a divorce.... We have been inseparable through the good and the bad. I can always depend on her.

To my dear friends Cheryl Dorsey and Robert Arguelles. who had enough faith in me to sow into my ministry. How can I say thanks for what you mean to me? I thank God for your obedience.

To my brother, the Late Reverend Hilliard Hudson, thank you for being that example of God's love. I can still hear your voice telling me that I can do it. I miss you so much. To my oldest brother Jammie, who was fearless and taught me how to always push forward. I will see you guys in heaven. To my younger sister Sammy and younger brother Mel, thanks for all your prayers. My brother, Elder Dale Hudson, thank you for pushing me to dig and dig into God's word to find and understand the golden nuggets that God has for us.

Last but not least, to my sons, Desmond and Evan. I love you more than words can describe. Thank you for all the times you listened and really didn't want to, but were obedient. I love you, buddies!

INTRODUCTION

Why do you think God created your mind? And why did he place the brain in your head instead of another part of your body? The brain is the most mysterious and little understood organ in the entire body. It's the source of our thoughts, our emotions, and our memories. Our brain is responsible for whatever conscious efforts we make. It's the original supercomputer. When a developing fetus is only four weeks old, its brain cells form at the rate of a quarter-million per minute. Without a brain to control the body, life wouldn't ever be possible.

Let's discuss it. I believe the brain was placed in your head because it's the top priority.

There is a story in the Bible about a group of people that put their brains together and decided to build a city and a tower tall enough to reach heaven. They began building and building. The Lord came down to see the city and the tower that the children of men were building. "And the Lord said, Behold, the people are one, and they have all one language; and this they begin to do: and now nothing will be restrained from them, which they imagined to do" (Gen. 11:6, King James 2000).

Let's think about this for a minute. The men believed that something could be done and put that belief into action, so much so that the Lord had to come down to see. Imagination is a very powerful tool that we have. We can imagine something and then meditate on it long enough to put it into action and actually achieve it.

CHAPTER 1

BELIEVING AND RECEIVING

A long time ago, God made an unbreakable promise that most people don't know about. This was done to ensure us that whatever we needed, he had for us. The promise is called a blood covenant. Children sometimes have a friend they love so much that they say, "Let's be friends forever and never part." So they prick their fingers, put them together, and say, "Now we are friends forever." So consider this true story about two men named David and Jonathan.

They were the best of friends, but Jonathan's father, Saul, became angry at David because of the women who danced and sang, saying, "Saul has slain thousands, and David ten thousand." Jonathan informed David of his father's anger, stating "My father wants to kill you, so please watch your back. Find a place to hide from my father." Jonathan also tried to smooth things over with his father and talk some sense into him. Eventually, Saul agreed not to kill David.

When another war broke out with the Philistines, David went to fight them. He struck them a mighty blow, and they fled from him. Instead of being a pleased king, Saul sought to pin David to the wall with his spear, but David slipped away. Saul drove the spear into the wall. So David fled and escaped that night. Jonathan still tried to make peace between his father and his friend. Saul got so angry with him that he threw a spear at Jonathan as he had done to David. Saul could not capture David, so he told his entire household how David hated them and if he got a chance, he would kill them all.

Jonathan later married and had a son by the name of Mephibosheth. When the boy was five, Jonathan and Saul were killed in the battle of Jezreel. This was terrible news. Not just because of their deaths, but because no one could stop David from coming in and taking over as king. People thought David was going to kill all the descendants of Saul and all those who were loyal to him; that he would punish the entire household and bring destruction to them. David had no intention of doing that. Saul had thought that was his plan, so he drilled that lie into them.

When the news of the deaths of Saul and Jonathan reached Jerusalem, Mephibosheth's nurse grabbed him and fled. In her hurry to get away, she fell and dropped Mephibosheth. As he hit the ground, both of his feet were crushed. She picked him up and carried him to a hideout east of the Jordan River called Lo-debar.

As he stayed in hiding in Lo-debar, every time Mephibosheth looked at his crushed feet, he was reminded that David wanted to kill him. Mephibosheth's hatred for David grew. David became king while Mephibosheth was hiding like a fugitive in fear of David. He has no idea there was a covenant between David and his father, Jonathan.

David reigned as king and asked if any of Saul's family was still around. No one replied because they thought it was a ploy, and that David was trying to find Mephibosheth to kill him. At last one of the servants told David about Mephibosheth, and that he lived in Lo-debar. Immediately, David sent his chariots out to get him. As Mephibosheth heard the sound of the chariots, a great fear came over him, for he thought David had found him and was going to kill him, as Saul had said. There was nothing he could do.

When David's chariots arrived, they rushed Mephibosheth to David. *Well, it's over for me now,* Mephibosheth thought. *When I get to David, he is going to torture me, behead me, and feed me to the dogs.* When they arrived to the palace, Mephibosheth fell on his face before David. David told him not to fear, "for I will surely show you kindness for

Jonathan your father's sake, and will restore to you all the land of Saul your father" (2 Sam. 9:7, World English Bible).

Mephibosheth was shocked because of all the things he had said and believed about David. He felt unworthy of all that David was doing for him. David informed him that it wasn't about him but was about the covenant he had made with Mephibosheth's father. David told Mephibosheth that he and all his descendants would live there with him in the palace, that Mephibosheth would be like David's son, he would take care of him, and Mephibosheth would never suffer lack again. This story is found in the Bible, in 1 and 2 Samuel.

This story is very close to the covenant God made concerning us. God made this binding agreement, but not with man, in the event that man would change his mind and go back on his promise, or would let something or someone talk him out of it. God could not and would not take a chance on that. God wanted it to be so tight that nothing or no one could touch it. As you know, in order for an agreement to be complete, there has to be a signature. The covenant was signed in Jesus's blood, which was shed on the cross at Calvary.

Just before Jesus died, he spoke three words: "It is finished." That is when the covenant went into effect. You can say that this is the will that is provided for us. A will or testament (covenant) is a legal declaration by which a person, the testator, names one or more persons to manage his or her estate and that provides for a distribution of his property at death. So now you get the picture. We have an inheritance.

> It's in Christ that we find out who we are and what we are living for. Long before we first heard of Christ and got our hopes up, he had his eye on us, had designs on us for glorious living, part of the overall purpose he is working out in everything and everyone. It's in Christ that you, once you heard the truth and believed it (this Message of your salvation), found yourselves home free—signed, sealed, and delivered by the Holy Spirit. This signet from God is the first installment on what's coming and a reminder that we'll get everything God has planned for us, a praising and glorious life (Eph. 1:11-14, The Message).

Sounds too good to be true, right? It's true. It's really true!

CHAPTER 2

THAT'S GREAT NEWS;
WHAT'S MY NEXT STEP?

If you confess with your mouth the Lord Jesus and believe in your heart that God raised him from the dead, you will be saved. "For with the heart man believeth unto righteousness, and with the mouth confession is made unto salvation" (Rom. 10: 10, KJV).What I am saying is that in order for you to take part in this inheritance, you have to belong to the family. You must accept Jesus as your personal savior. You don't have to jump over hoops or anything, just accept him in your heart. By doing so, your life will have new meaning. You will never be alone, because God said he will never leave you.

As you develop your relationship with him (Jesus), he will help you in all the decisions you have to make. One thing is for sure—you have to trust him. Proverbs 3:5 (The Message) states, "Trust God from the bottom of your heart [with all your heart]; don't try to figure out everything on your own." Listen for God's voice in everything you do, everywhere you go. He's the one who will keep you on track. Don't assume that you know it all. Run to God, run from evil!

When I was a little girl, my siblings and I would play a game of trust. There were seven of us, and when it rained or our parents had gone out, we would play in the house. We would pretend to faint, and the others had to catch us before we hit the floor. One of my brothers was such a prankster, he would wait until I was almost on the floor before he would catch me. Of course that would freak me out, but he would never let me fall.

Jesus is our big brother, and there may be times when it seems as if he is not there. Keep the faith. He will never let you fall. Jesus loves us so much, more than we can ever fathom. Just think about it: he died for us, he was beaten, mocked, kicked, spit upon, and stripped of his clothes. What he went through was brutal. They nailed him on the cross, where he bled and died. It was all for us. Everything was for our healing. He died so that we may live. He took our sorrow that we may have joy; he took unrighteousness so that we may be made righteous; he took our brokenness so that we would be made whole; he endured hate so that we would have love. In times of disappointments he gave us hope. Who wouldn't love Jesus for that? Now that is true love. And what did we do to deserve all that? Nothing!

The point I am making is that it's not about what we do or have done. It's about what he has done for us. He took all—and I mean all—of our unrighteousness and made us righteous. Maybe you are asking if all the good that comes to you is because of what Jesus did. Yes, that is exactly what I am saying. The question that comes to my mind is, Why do people fear? Another is, Why after all that do people doubt? I John 4:18 (American King James Version) says: "There is no fear in love; but perfect love casts out fear: because fear has torment. He that fears is not been made perfect in love." God is Love.

When we take up permanent residence in a life of love, we live in God and God lives in us. This way, love has the run of the house. It becomes at home and matures in us, so that we are free of worry on Judgment Day. Our standing in the world is identical with Christ's. There is no room in love for fear. Well-formed love banishes fear. Since fear is crippling, a fearful life that is filled with fear of death and fear of judgment is a life that is not yet fully formed in love. We are going to love and be loved. First we were loved, now we love.

God loved us first. If anyone boasts "I love God" and goes right on hating his brother or sister, thinking nothing of it, he is a liar. If he won't love the person he can see, how can he love God, whom he can't see? The command we have from Christ is very blunt: loving God includes loving people. You have got to love both. I Corinthians13:13 (New King James Version)—"And now abide faith, hope, love, these three; but the greatest of these is love."

"Trust in the Lord with all your heart, and lean not to your own understanding; In all your ways acknowledge Him and He shall direct your paths" (Prov. 3:5-6, NKJV).

CHAPTER 3

TIME—OUR TIME OR SET TIME

I have two sons. I wanted a girl, but I stopped at the boys. When they were young, they played football, so I was forced to learn the game. This chapter makes me think of football.

When I watched the game, I noticed something. When the team got in a huddle a play was given. The play was created by the coach and given to the quarterback to be passed on to the other players. The play was the instruction for the players' action. If it was followed correctly, the team would get closer to its goal. Another thing, the players couldn't be out of position. If it was a pass play. the quarterback threw the ball not to the wide receiver, but to the spot where the wide receiver was supposed to be. If he was there he could catch the ball; if not, he would miss it.

Using my imagination, I recast the football game. The coach represents God, the play is his word (which is Jesus), the quarterback is the Holy Spirit, and we are the wide receivers. We receive the word and the Holy Spirit gives us the power. But we have to be in position in order to receive the blessing, after which we run with it. Let us not forget that the enemy will always try to stop us and block us. He will do all he can, even double-team us, but we have to know without a shadow of a doubt that "greater is he that is within you, than he that is in the world" (1 John 4:4, KJV). Additionally, "No weapon that is formed against you shall prosper, and every tongue which rises against you in judgment you shall condemn. This is the heritage of the servants of the Lord, and their righteousness is from Me, says the Lord" (Isaiah 54:17, NKJV).

We often feel that God works in our time. In reality, God created time, so time has to obey God. He has a set time for everything. We have to stay in position so that when the time comes for our change, we won't be waiting at the bus stop when we should be at the airport. We must obey the Lord when he speaks. He will speak when we need a word. He will either speak to us directly, send someone to us with a word from him, or he will direct us to his word. There have been times when God has sent an angel or communicated through a dream.

God has so many ways to get his message across. That's why we need to take the limits off him. God is limitless. There are many stories in the Bible when God does things that, to us, make no sense. In 1 Kings 17, there is a story about the prophet Elijah, who proclaimed that there would be no dew nor rain except by his word. After he had proclaimed that, the Lord told Elijah to go eastward and hide by the brook called Cherith, which flowed into the Jordan. He was to drink from the brook, and God said that he would send him food to eat, though not by a man or a woman. God said that he would send it by a raven. Yes, I said a raven. God commanded the ravens to bring Elijah bread and meat in the morning and the evening. Ravens are known to steal food from other birds, mammals, and dogs. They follow hunters and fishermen long enough to steal from them. Wow! Just think. God chose a raven to bring bread and meat to the prophet, and the raven didn't eat the food, but followed God's instructions. Now, if a bird can obey God, then man with his intelligent mind can understand all the benefits of obeying God, following God's plan for his life, and receiving all the things that God has made possible for him. God loved us so much that he sent his son to die for us. He created this Earth for us and gave us instructions on how to receive his best and live our best.

You may say, Well, there are so many things that I need. Where are they? God said in his word that you have not because you ask not. Okay, so you may say, I want God to give me one million dollars. Don't be silly. You know you don't have million-dollar faith when you can't believe God to pay your phone bill. You have to start where your Faith is. Rom. 12:3 (NKJV): "God has dealt to each one a measure of faith." You have the faith. To have stronger faith, you have to hear the word of God. Rom.10:17 (NKJV): "So then faith comes by hearing, and hearing the word of God." You have to hear the word (the Bible), and then you will see that you will grow stronger daily as you hear God's word. You can even hear yourself read the Bible aloud. It's like eating, except you are feeding your spirit. You don't feed your body once a week, or once a month. If that were the case, you would become very weak. You have to feed your spirit just like you feed your body. On a daily basis.

Matthew 7:7-11 (NKJV) says:

> Ask, and it shall be given you; seek, and you shall find; knock, and it will be opened to you. For everyone who asks receives, and he who seeks finds, and to him who knocks it will be opened. Or what man is there among you who, if his son asks for bread, will give him a stone? Or if he asks for a fish, will give him a serpent? If you then, being evil, know how to give good gifts to your children, how much more will

your Father who is in heaven give good things
to those who ask Him!

Sounds simple, right? It is, but we make it difficult. Ask, seek, knock = ASK! John 15:16 (NKJV) says: "You did not choose me, but I chose you, and appointed you that you should go and bear fruit, and that your fruit should remain, that whatever you ask the Father in My name He may give you."

CHAPTER 4

FORGIVENESS

What can I say? We all have had to do this from time to time. Let me share some stories with you.

I have a friend, whose name I will change to Darla. She went around singing at different churches and functions. One day she sang at a meeting, and after it was over a young man approached her. She thought he was kind of cute. He said, "I really enjoyed your singing." She thanked him. After that, it seemed that everywhere she went to sing, he would show up. She would think, *There's that guy again.* Somehow or another, he would find a way to her to speak to her. She would try to dodge him by losing him in a crowd, but she was not fast enough. One day she was on her way back to her hotel after singing at a conference, and guess who she met at the front of the hotel? That same guy. She spoke to him and he gave her a big smile and answered.

She found out that his name was Jerry. She decided to talk to him more to see what he was about. She found out he was a very nice guy. They began to communicate via long-distance phone calls, letters, etc. They became very close, and the closeness turned into love. Darla was so head over hills for Jerry, she wanted to move to the same city he was in, but not until he asked her to marry him.

She waited, and one day while they were talking on the phone it happened. Jerry asked her to marry him—over the phone and without a ring. Darla moved to the city where he lived, and he made the arrangements for her to live with an older lady named Ms. Lou (not her real name). Darla frequently spent the night with Jerry, and this went on for two years. Finally Darla thought that this was getting old, so she asked him, "When are we going to get married?" His response was, "I'm not good enough for you, you deserve better."

Needless to say, Darla thought she knew him and thought this was only a mind game. So she cried and said, "I love you!" This went on, and things changed. He would get angry at her for no reason. All she knew was church, but he knew the streets. So he got control over her. Darla became filled with fear. She started to pray and cry out to God. She got her answer. God told her to go, but she chose to stay. God gives us free will. We can obey him or do things our way. After the two years, they were married. Jerry borrowed his sister's ring set for the wedding and he still didn't buy Darla a ring. Many bad things happened to her throughout the marriage including abuse, both mental and physical.

This went on for twenty-five years. Jerry played mind games that created fear, so much fear that Darla was not able to think clearly. When she had had enough, Darla made up her mind that she was going to trust God no matter what. She was too embarrassed to talk to her family and friends. She put all of her trust in God and his word. She listened to God and did everything he instructed her to do. She left Jerry and started a new, happy, and fulfilled life, yet there was something the enemy was holding over her head—forgiveness. Darla had to forgive Jerry, and herself.

She wanted to say, "Lord make him pay for what he did to me, for all the years I've lost. Make him pay for the pain caused me!" She wanted a happy marriage, but this is not God's way. She had to forgive Jerry, she had to forgive herself for not obeying God, and she had to ask God to forgive her. Mark 11:25 (English Standard Version) says, "And whenever you stand praying, forgive, if you have anything against anyone, so that your Father also who is in heaven may forgive you your trespasses." 1 Cor. 10:13 (ESV) says: "No temptation has overtaken you that is not common to man. God is faithful, and he will not let you be tempted beyond your ability, but with the temptation he will also provide the way to escape, that you may be able to endure it."

God was with Darla through it all. He offered her help, but she was not ready to accept it. God waited until she had had enough. Yes, God was there all the time, waiting on her as he is waiting on us. Darla finally forgave Jerry and is able to pray for him. Also, she has released all the fear in her life and replaced it with faith. She forgave herself and asked God to forgive her and make her over. She now has a wonderful life. She had to change the way she was thinking; she had to say what God said about her. She had to have the mind of Christ and the wisdom of God.

If we continue to listen to what the enemy is saying to us, he will destroy us and all our dreams and visions. Psalms 37:4-5 (NKJV) states, "Delight yourself also in the Lord, and He shall give you the desires of your heart. Commit your way to the Lord, trust also in him and He shall bring it to pass." Are there times in your life when you wanted to have do-overs? You thought of the mistakes you've made, wrong decisions followed by wrong actions. As a result, you began to feel awful. This is the first step for the enemy to move in and get into your head. He will start to tell you what a loser you are and how stupid you have been. This will go on and on until you are so depressed that you start to feel worthless. We can't get into the habit of listening to the enemy.

Remember, the enemy comes to do only three things: to kill, steal, and destroy. He can do only what you allow him to do. The sole power he has to use against you is the power you give him. Yes, God has given you authority over your life. You can choose to listen to all the negative things the enemy has to say to you, or you can choose not to listen to his foolishness. Forgive those who have hurt you, forgive yourself. Stop listening to the false accusations. Another name for the enemy is the accuser of the brethren. Not only men, but women too. The devil is not capable of telling the truth. He will lie and deceive, and then destroy. God wants us to heed his word, follow his teaching, love those that hate us, pray, and forgive those who misuse and abuse us.

Don't lose your grip on love and loyalty. Tie them around your neck; carve their initials on your heart. Earn a reputation for living well in God's eyes and the eyes of people. Trust God from the bottom of your heart and don't try to figure out everything on your own. Listen to God's voice in everything you do, everywhere you go. He's the one who will keep you on track. Don't assume that you know it all. As I noted earlier, Prov. 3:6 (NKJV) states, "In all your ways acknowledge [God], and He shall direct your paths."

I will end this chapter with a definition of the word acknowledge. This word is defined as: to admit to be real or true; recognizes the existence, truth, or fact of, preserve. Just something to think about.

CHAPTER 5

START FROM WHERE YOU ARE!

Are you ready? Chapters one through four gave you information on what you need to know. We must accept Jesus as our Savior, develop a relationship with him, renew our minds daily with the word of God, and believe in him. Don't doubt, for if you doubt, you will do without. So in order to receive, you must believe and follow his word, not stray from it, and forgive. Most of all, know that he loves us more than anything. That's why he sent his only begotten son into the world to die for us, so that we would have life everlasting, abundant life, which means all our needs supplied. What I am saying is that we are living in the *finished work of Jesus Christ.*

Okay, stop thinking, *Now I have to go to church more, pray more, witness more, fast more. I was fasting once a week; now I have to increase it to three times a week. Stop watching TV, etc.* Those are things that religion has taught, not what God has taught. Remember the title of this book? Change your thinking, change your life. If you are thinking like that, it is time to change."

> For by grace you have been saved through faith; and that not of yourselves; it is the gift of God, not of works, lest anyone should boast (Eph. 2:8-9, NKJV).

What this is saying is there is nothing you can do because it has already been done for you. It says: "not of works, lest anyone should boast." You know how people are. They will try to get brownie points from God by doing more works, paying more money in church, helping more people in need, showing God what good Christians they are, showing God that they are more worthy than others. But there is nothing you can do or say. Everything that needed to be done was in the finished work of Christ.

I have a friend named Shay who would not ask God for anything. Nor would she believe he would help her, because of all the things she had done in her life. She felt that he was angry with her for all those things, and that if she tried to talk to him, he would bring up all of the wrong she had done. I had to tell her, and I am telling you, that God is not angry at her. He loves her and wants her to come to him for all her needs.

God is love. God is good all the time, and all the time God is good. Satan wants you to think all those wrong thoughts about God because he wants you to believe that what you've done in your life is unforgivable. That is wrong thinking and wrong believing. God's grace for you is endless and his love for you is everlasting. That is the only way God wants you to think. He has forgiven you of all your sins.

Now what is it you want from the Lord? What do you need? What do you want out of life? What do you want for your family? God said, if you can believe it, you can achieve it. In the next chapter, let me help you start this journey of love with Jesus!

CHAPTER 6

NEVER GIVE UP!

I know that now that you have all this information, you are ready to start your journey, or you have more fuel for the journey. When you figure out what you want the Lord to help you achieve in life, these are the steps. But before you start, let me tell you a story about me.

I realized that God was with me all along; that he wanted to help me and lead me to my destiny, and most of all, how much he loved me. All I could do was thank him and cry. No one had ever expressed love like that to me before. Just think—God only had one son, and he loved me so much that he sent his son to be a sacrifice for me (and you), without us doing a thing for it. He wanted me to have the best in life. Wow! And his son knew that was his purpose for coming into the world, unlike Abraham and Isaac.

God told Abraham to take his son, whom he loved, to the land of Moriah and offer him as a burnt sacrifice (offering). Isaac also was the son of Sarah, who did not get pregnant until she was ninety years old. This was her only child. Yet Abraham was obedient to God and was going to offer Isaac up to God. Abraham told no one of what God told him to do.

> So Abraham rose early in the morning and saddled his donkey, and took two of his young men with him, and Isaac his son; and he split the wood for the burnt offering, and arose and went to the place of which God had told him (Gen. 22:3).

Can you imagine what was going through Abraham's mind, knowing what he was about to do? And what was he going to tell Sarah, his wife? After he arrived at the place on the third day:

> Abraham said to his young men, "Stay here with the donkey; the lad and I will go yonder and worship, and we will come back to you." So Abraham took the wood for the burnt offering and laid it on Isaac his son; and he took the fire in his hand, and the knife, and the two of them went up together. But Isaac spoke to his father and said … "Look, the fire and the wood, but

where is the lamb for the burnt offering? And Abraham said, "My son, God will provide for Himself the lamb for the burnt offering." So they two of them went together. Then they came to the place of which God had told him. And Abraham built an altar there and placed the wood in order; and he bound Isaac his son and laid him on the altar, upon the wood. And Abraham stretched out his hand and took the knife to slay his son. But the Angel of the Lord called to him from heaven and said, "Abraham, Abraham!" So he said, "Here I am." And He said, "Do not lay your hand on the lad, or do anything to him; for now I know that you fear God, since you have not withheld your son, your only son, from Me." Then Abraham lifted his eyes and looked, and there behind him was a ram caught in the thicket by his horns. So Abraham went and took the ram, and offered it for a burnt offering instead of his son (Gen. 22:5-13).

As you read the remainder of this story, you will see that God tells Abraham that because of his obedience, he and his descendants will be blessed. God did not have Abraham to sacrifice his son, because God does not approve of human sacrifices. And whatever we will need, God said he will provide.

Even when you can't see your way clear, keep trusting God. He surely will provide whatever you are in need of, and he is always on time. Never give up! Never give in! Keep trusting God, and then you will always win. You must be persistent.

There is a story in the Bible of a woman who was very sick. She had an issue of blood for twelve years. Back then, when that time of the month came for women, they were not allowed in public, yet this woman had bled for twelve years. She had suffered many things, had visited many physicians, and had spent all that she had. She didn't feel better, but rather grew worse. She heard people talking about Jesus and made up in her mind that if she could get to him, even just to touch his garment, that she would be made whole. A women in her condition, who was weak and did not want to go out in public for fear of what could happen to her, made up her mind that she was going to get to Jesus no matter what. I can just see her, crawling at times, so weak she almost fainted, yet determined to be made whole. She probably knew she couldn't get close enough to him to have him lay hands on her, but if she could touch his garment, she would get her healing and could go home. Well, she did get close enough to touch the hem of his garment, and having such great faith, what she believed would happen did. Straightway the fountain of her blood was dried up, and she felt in her body that she was healed of the plague.

Jesus, immediately knowing that virtue had gone out of him, turned about in the pressing crowd and said, "Who touched me?"

> But His disciples said to Him, "You see the multitude thronging You, and You say, 'Who touched Me?'" And he looked around and saw her. But the woman, fearing and trembling, knowing what had happened to her, came and fell down before Him and told Him the whole truth. And He said to her, "Daughter, your faith has made you well. Go in peace, and be whole of your affliction" (Mark 5:31-34, NKJV).

Here we see the faith of this woman, who had faith and works. She believed that she could touch Jesus's clothes and be healed. All odds were against her, yet she never gave up. She could have given up, considering her condition and knowing what the people could do to her. She could have just said, I have nothing to live for, I've spent all I have, I'm getting worse, I'm tired, and I don't know what else to do. That was not the case, because she had heard of all the good things Jesus was doing and she wanted to be a part of that. She never gave up! When Jesus said to her, "Go in peace, and be whole of your affliction," I believe that not only was she healed, but her entire life was renewed. She went to him sick, weak, and broke. I believed when she left, all her needs were filled.

When God gives you what you ask for, he gives you more than enough, never just enough. Glory to God! This is an example of what being persistent in whatever you desire from God can do. You say it, see it, believe it, and you will achieve it. I Corinthians 15:58 (The Message) says: With all this going for us, my dear, dear friends, stand your ground. And don't hold back. Throw yourselves in to the work of the Master, confident that nothing you do for him is a waste of time of effort." I also like the King James Version. It reads: "Therefore, my beloved brethren, be ye stedfast, unmoveable, always abounding in the work of the Lord, forasmuch as ye know that your labor is not in vain in the Lord." God has everything you need!

CHAPTER 7

SO, HOW IS YOUR THINKING?

Are you really ready for a changed life? Okay, let's start with this, Proverbs 23:7 (NKJV): "For as he thinks in his heart, so is he." Your thinking is very important. As you renew your mind daily with the word of God, your thinking is also renewed. It's an easy thing to do. You will find that the more you read and meditate on the word of God, the more your worries seem not that serious.

I am speaking from experience. Since I have been meditating on the word of God, I have entered into his rest. This did not happen overnight; it took a while. I would say, I am going to trust God and really mean it. Yet I would always find myself looking at the situations and circumstances that caused unbelief to enter in my mind, weakening my faith and strengthening doubt and its cousin, unbelief. I would always wonder why it was taking so long for me to receive from God.

When God told Abraham and his wife Sarah that they were going to have a son in their old age, and even that he would become the father of all nations, Abraham held fast to the word of God. In Rom. 4:18-21 (KJV):

> Who against hope believed in hope, that he might become the father of many nations; according to that which was spoken so shall thy seed be. And being not weak in faith, he considered not his own body now dead, when he was about an hundred years old, neither yet the deadness of Sarah's womb: He staggered not at the promise of God through unbelief; but was strong in faith, giving Glory to God. And being fully persuaded that, what God had promised, he was able to perform.

This is saying that we have to hold fast to God's word *only*. Just as Abraham did. He did not consider his age, the condition of his body, nor the age of his wife and the condition of her body. He only considered the promise of God. That's how we receive. We have to be fully persuaded and not waver. We cannot be moved by what we see, hear, want, or feel. The enemy will always show us the situation, and even have credible people talk to us, trying to shake our faith. I will say it again: Do not consider the condition, don't consider the situation. Keep your mind on the promise of God!

We must rest in the finished work of Jesus Christ. A lot of people say, How can I rest? Can't you see all this? You are still considering the problem. You can't do that when you trust God's word. I know it's slapping you in your face. Remember: "greater is he that is in you, than he that is in the world" (1 John 4:4, KJV). 2 Cor. 2:14 (KJV) says: "Now thanks be unto God, which always causeth us to triumph in Christ, and maketh manifest the savour of his knowledge by us in every place."

Yes! We always win! Always! Knowing this, we can rest. Let's look at the word *rest*. It means: "to cease work or movement in order to relax, refresh oneself, or recover strength, be placed or supported so as to stay in a specified position, an instance or period of relaxing or ceasing to engage in strenuous or stressful activity. An object that is used to support something." Heb. 4:9-11 (KJV) says:

> There remaineth therefore a rest to the people of God. For he that is entered into his rest, he also hath ceased from his own works, as God did from his. Let us labor therefore to enter into that rest, lest any man fall after the example of unbelief.

This is what I began to apply to my life. I entered into God's rest. I surly could not do anything about the issue. I gave it to God and just began to rest. Rest in knowing that God was taking care of it all. Did it come to my mind? Yes. Did I give it a place in my mind? No! I just began to praise God for handling the issue, giving all glory to God. Sometimes I would speak out loud, saying what God said. Meditating more on the word of God, waiting for the manifestation. And it will surely manifest, because you are feeding your faith and starving you doubts to death. "Trust in the Lord with all thine heart; and lean not unto thine own understanding. In all thy ways acknowledge him, and he shall direct thy paths (Prov. 3:5-6 KJV).

CHAPTER 8

IT'S TIME FOR DECISION MAKING

Now that you have read chapters one through seven, keeping in mind the title of this book, do you need an extra thought? Okay I will give you one. In Matt. 7:24-27 (NKJV) you will find that extra thought.

> "Therefore whoever hears these sayings of Mine, and does them, I will liken him to a wise man who built his house on the rock: and the rain descended, the flood came, and the winds blew and beat on that house; and it did not fall, for it was founded on the rock. But everyone who hears these sayings of Mine, and does not do them, will be like a foolish man who built his house on the sand: and the rain descended, the floods came, and the winds blew and beat on the house; and it fell, and great was its fall."

You may say to yourself, Wow, what a story. You may think that Jesus is the rock. The wise man built on Jesus, and the foolish man built on the sand, which was not the rock. That's a good answer, but you are missing the point. Some may say that you must have a strong foundation for whatever you start in order for it to succeed. Well, that is also a good answer, but you are not yet there.

Now, I will tell you the point that I am making. At the beginning of this passage, it says: "'Therefore, whoever hears these sayings of Mine, and does them …'" It also says, "'… everyone who hears these sayings of Mine, and does not do them …'" When you study God's word and begin to apply his sayings to your life, to walk in them daily, you are then a doer. But when you hear the words and Jesus's instructions concerning your life and do not apply them, you are considered a hearer only. That is the message I'm trying to convey. God has a perfect plan for your life that you will take part in only if you follow his instructions. Don't just be a hearer, which will get you nowhere, as it did the foolish man. Be a doer of the word and there will be no limits on what you can achieve with God. We serve a God of *no limits*. By following him and being a doers of his word, we too have no limits.

With God all things are possible to them that believe. *Can't* is no such thing with God. With that being said, what are your dreams, what are your desires? God will turn your impossibilities into possibilities, your lack into more than enough. Where you are weak, he will make you strong. He will turn your fear into faith, your *I can't* into *I can*, your *I need* into *I have*, your *I am sick* to *I am healed*, you discouragement into *I am encouraged*. I can go on and on, but I think you get the picture. This is a daily walk, and it will get brighter and brighter to those that are doers of the word.

The days of the week are seven. Sunday through Saturday. Now, if you eat a good, nourishing meal on Sunday, will it keep you through the remainder of the week? No. You have to feed your body daily. In most cases, you are ready to eat a few hours after Sunday's meal. That is how a lot of us treat our spirits. After leaving church on Sunday, we don't even pick up the Bible until the next Sunday, when the pastor says, "Open your Bibles to …" There has to be a change. If you keep getting the same results by doing the same things, it's time to change.

Different and better actions will guarantee better results. If you are tired of the same old same old, and you desperately want and need a change, change your *thinking*. By doing that, you will *change your life!*

MY BIO

Believe Ministries was formed by Vanessa Clark as a result of her time in intimate worship and years of Bible study. This journey started years earlier, when Vanessa began singing in church at an early age. She became the minister in music at her father's church, St. Paul Missionary Baptist, in Decatur, Illinois. The church was a part of the Woodriver Baptist District Association, where Vanessa served as music director of a four-hundred voice youth choir. She also served as music director of the Illinois State Congress of Christian Education, with an eight-hundred voice youth choir. While living in Illinois, Vanessa conducted music workshops for various organizations, including the Illinois State University gospel choir.

During this time, Vanessa's father called the church to forty days of prayer and fasting. On the seventh day of the fast, the Lord spoke to Vanessa and said, "Strengthen your brother." She pondered the word she had received from the Lord as she continued in the music ministry.

In the early 1980s, Vanessa moved to Memphis, Tennessee, and became a member of the Temple of Deliverance Cathedral of Bountiful Blessings, founded by the late Bishop G. E. Patterson. She organized the youth choir and traveled with Bishop Patterson as a member of his crusade team, ministering in song. Opportunities opened for Vanessa to record with various artists such as the Reverend Al Green, Elder Richard (Mr. Clean) White. On occasions she sang and traveled with Dewitt Johnson, Myrna Summers, Tramaine Hawkins, and the late Reverend James Cleveland.

She was even afforded the opportunity of singing at the Grand Ole Opry in Nashville, Tennessee. After relocating to Detroit, Michigan, she continued in the music ministry, both singing and training choirs. There she sang with artists such as Karen Clark Sheard, Dorinda Clark Cole, and recorded with the Craig Bothers.

Although Vanessa studied the word of God throughout her years of music ministry, a time arose when she truly fell in love with the word of God like never before. The Lord gave her a love for the word that was so strong, she devoted all her attention to preparing for teaching and ministering. It was at this time that the Lord reminded

Vanessa of the words he'd spoken over twenty years before: "Strengthen your brother." However, the words had new meaning. She realized the Lord had, over time, birthed in her a vision to reach out and share the word with people all over the world, and to strengthen them with their walk with Christ throughout their everyday lives. From this, I Believe Ministries was born. Vanessa moved from not only sharing the ministry in song, but to preaching and teaching as well.

On one particular occasion, the Lord opened doors for her to minister to the Chicagoland Women's Conference, where he manifested his presence and power in an awesome way. Beyond her study of the word of God, Vanessa gained additional insight and Biblical knowledge from Charis Bible School, founded by Andrew Womack; Benjamin Gilbert, bishop and pastor of Detroit World Outreach Christian Church, in Redford, Michigan; and Elder Dale Hudson, Covenant Word Ministries. After twenty-eight years at FedEx, Vanessa has retired and resides in Houston, Texas. The Lord has led her to be a part of the Joan Hunter Ministries, known as the Joint Heirs in the Miraculous.

You can visit Vanessa's website at:
www.ibelieveministry.org.

TESTIMONY

I know you are wondering where the thought for this book came from. Years ago I went through a horrific experience, and I needed to hear from God for guidance and wisdom. I knew God was always there; I just didn't acknowledge him. I kept looking for an experience like the one Moses had. You know, take me up to a mountain and speak to me. Or the three Hebrew men that were placed in the fiery furnace; or Daniel when he was placed in the lion's den. Well, that didn't happen.

At one time I got upset with God, saying, "I know you see what I am going through. When you are going to step in?" I heard nothing. I went back to the word of God and read and studied. After that I said, "Lord, I know you can help me, I know that you helped the others. Am I doing something I shouldn't be doing, or am I not doing something I should be doing? Help me out here, God? What's up, God?"

I never gave up. I keep searching, praying, going to church, singing, doing good works, yet there was no change. I thought that if I did not cuss, drink, smoke, do drugs, or go to the clubs, God would notice and come to my rescue me. You know, like a damsel in distress. I never was unfaithful to my husband, I was the best wife I could be, and I was the best mother I could be to my sons. What was holding up my blessings?

I read a passage in the Bible that said we are not saved by works. Wow, I thought. That's what I was doing. Then I learned about the two covenants, the old one—which is called law—and the new one, which is called grace. The old covenant was going on before Christ was born. In order for people to receive forgiveness for their sins, they had to offer a burnt sacrifice. This was when the Ten Commandments were in full effect. The old covenant was given to the Jews. Of course, I am not living in that time. There is no need for me to make a burnt sacrifice for the forgiveness of my sins, so that does not apply. In those times, a person could not go the Father on her own; she had to go through a priest. In the book of Luke, there is a story about a man called Zacharias who was a priest, and he would go before the Lord in the temple on behalf of the people. He would go behind a veil and pray to God. This was in the time called BC—before Christ.

The new covenant, grace, is the dispensation of Jesus Christ, given to the Gentiles. Jesus came because the people could not keep the law. They needed help that no one could give but Jesus. He came to show us a better way to live and to receive the best that this world could offer. Jesus was, and is, the way, the only way to the Father. By his death on the cross, he gave us his righteousness, so that the old way of receiving forgiveness for our sins was obsolete. Through his death on the cross, the veil was torn, letting us know that there is no longer a need to go through a priest to talk to him.

Grace through faith will get his attention, not works that any man can boast of. Everything was finished at the cross. Jesus Christ is standing at the door of your heart knocking, asking if he can come in. If you let him in, he said that he would come in and sup with you. Meaning, he will come in and have the main meal with you to fill up, to render, to supply, to fulfill, to occupy. What am I saying is, once you let Jesus in, he will fulfill all your needs.

That is God's grace. Such a simple thing to do. I had to fully commit to him, trust him with no wavering. Peter did it when he stepped out of the boat to walk to Jesus. When he started to fear, he started to sink. I had to see his example and see through it. That means, once you accept Jesus fully and totally, you can't let anyone or anything get between you and what God has prepared for you. You have to keep your eyes on the prize. Yes, winds will blow, trials will come, and you will have opposition. All that will make you doubt God and yourself. At times like those, you need to be like Abraham. You can't even consider the opposition that is coming against you, which are doubt, fear, and disbelief. Keep your eyes on Jesus. His word says that he will never leave you, nor will he forsake you. Remember that when you opened the door of your heart to him, he entered and took up residency to meet every need, to help you in every trial, in every storm, in every attack of the enemy. He let me know that greater is he that is in me (Jesus) than he (the devil) that is in the world. Once you have Jesus, you have more than enough. Always remember, Christ in you is the hope of glory! Never forget that. Now I know that Jesus is always with me.

I will always have victory in every situation, in every trial, in every storm. There was a song a while ago that stated "say to opposition, through your best shot." But I say, don't bother, because you will not win. I will win because God always causes me to triumph! So I say to you, we live in a time when *almost* is just not good enough. Winning always feels great. We are winners with Christ. There is no hard work involved. He is knocking at the door of your heart right now, saying, "Let me in. I will be with you, I will help you, I won't misuse you. I will lift you up when you are down. I will protect you and direct you. I will lead you and guide you. I will bless you and I will always be with you, no matter what. You can count on me!"

Jesus's death on the cross provided us with righteousness. He took all sorrows, guilt, and shame, all our mishaps, all our disappointments, our failures, our hurts. They were all nailed on the cross. Just help yourself out of all this. Accept Jesus as your personal Savior. All he wants to do is to make your life better than ever. Don't you think it's time?

I do and I did! Now I have the perfect relationship, which is the life in Christ. I am no longer alone, no longer depressed. Every day with Jesus is a brand-new experience, when I can enjoy the love of Jesus. When I open my eyes in the morning, I look forward to spending time with him. There is no longer a need for me to try to do things to get his attention, to show him what a good Christian I have become. He already knows, because I have accepted him into my heart. I believe every word he says, for all his promises to me are *yes* and *amen*. He has shown me on many, many occasions that if I would only trust him and never doubt, he would always bring me out. He has taught me to rest in the finished work of Christ.

Some of the last words he spoke on the cross were, "It is finished." I now know fully what that means. All the work has been done for us. All we have to do is believe and receive it. That's all. There is nothing we can add to what he has done, because he has done it all. We just believe, because he did the work. Acknowledge him in all your ways and he will direct your paths. Trust in him and he will bring it to pass. He loves it when we trust him. He has so many blessing for us. He just wants to shower us with good things, solely for our enjoyment, because he loves us so much. There are times that he blesses me with things I didn't ask for. I say, "Thank you, Jesus. You did that for me." He will answer, "Yes, I did, just because I love you." There is nothing like just-because blessings. Won't you join me? You will live your best life ever. Nothing is better than to live for Christ!

Printed in the United States
By Bookmasters